Remembering Ann through her Rhythm and Rhyme

A Collection of Poems and Short Stories written by Ann M. Lilley

By: Ann M. Lilley & Brenda L. Galeles

ISBN 978-1-105-53881-0

Published in the USA by Brenda L. Galeles at lulu.com

INTRODUCTION

My name is Brenda L. Galeles (maiden name Lilley). I am publishing this book on behalf of my sister Ann M. Lilley. Ann passed away on August 23, 2011, at the age of 53.

Ann resided in Wisconsin Rapids, Wisconsin, for the majority of her life. People living in or near Ann's hometown I am sure are familiar with her writing. But I am taking this opportunity to share with fellow readers everywhere a compilation of Ann's magic with words.

It was always Ann's dream to have her Chores and Snores short stories and poems turned into children's books, and her other poetry published as a book. That is why I decided to put all of her writing together and create this book.

I had always admired Ann for her courage, strength, endless source of creativity and never losing her sense of humor.

To Ann, With Love

CONTENTS

CHORES AND SNORES SHORT STORIES

The Adventure Story, The Missing Lunch and The Other Side of the Fence are short stories about Chores the farmer and his lazy dog Snores. In the following stories, Snores the dog is lazy but brave, just plain hungry and playful but messy. But regardless, Chores always finds him lovable.

Suitable for children

Ann wrote the following short stories between 1994 and 1997.

CHORES AND SNORES
THE ADVENTURE STORY

On a small farm in Wisconsin, Clint Andrews (known as Chores) keeps himself busy with a daily routine of milking cows, cleaning the barn and working in the fields.

Many farmers have cats and dogs on their farms because cats are good mousers and dogs will go out and bring the cows in all by themselves if taught to do so. This makes things much easier for the farmer.

Chores has countless cats lurking around on his farm. He often gets a glimpse of them peeping through the tall grass or scurrying about outside the milk house as they anxiously await a platter of fresh milk.

Along with his many cats, Chores also has a dog on his farm, an old Irish setter known as Snores. Unlike most dogs, Snores does not care to go on brisk walks or fetch a stick and he most definitely will not bring the cows in. He simply prefers to spend most of his time relaxing in his favorite spot, drifting in and out of sleep.

Chores says that the only thing wrong with Snores is that he is just plain lazy. The local veterinarian has checked Snores over several times. He too says that the dog is just plain lazy and that the name Snores is most appropriate for him.

Of course, there are times when even the laziest of dogs have to get up, stretch their legs and eat. It is during these times that Snores tends to stir up a little trouble and get into mischief.

He recently wandered into the chicken coop with Chores and managed to create some trouble in there. Chores had gone in and started gathering eggs as usual, gently placing them into a bucket. Snores stood there watching for a moment and decided to pitch in and help. He reached into one of the lower nests and pulled out an egg. Carefully grasping it in his mouth, he walked over to the bucket and dropped it in, breaking it on top of the other eggs.

Chores had his back turned at the time and he did not hear the egg break because the coop was full of clucking hens. He was quite surprised when he walked over to the bucket and looked inside. It was obvious what had happened, since that was not the first time that Snores had attempted to help gather the eggs.

Snores can be mischievous and lazy, but he is also somewhat of a hero. It was just late last spring that he saved a calf from nearly drowning by pulling it from a flooded creek.

Chores says it was a day that he will never

forget. The creek that runs behind the farm was flooding into the nearby pasture and a storm was fast approaching. He thought it would be a good idea to bring the cows in early, so he jumped into his truck and headed out to the pasture. Snores rode with him because storms make him restless and he always enjoys a ride in the truck.

Many of the cows were already on their way to the barn, but the rest of them needed a little coaxing. Rain was soon pouring down and thunder rumbled across the sky.

Molly the calf had become frightened and ran off, headed toward the creek. Chores took a rope from his truck and went after her, but she was running much too fast. He could not get close enough to get the lasso around her. The poor calf fell into the rapid current of the flooded creek.

It looked as though poor Molly was destined for disaster as she flowed downstream in the rushing water. With Snores at his side, Chores ran along the creek trying desperately to keep her in sight. He was starting to lose hope when Snores suddenly plunged into the water. He has always been a good swimmer but this was a real challenge for him. When he caught up to Molly, he grabbed onto her tail with his mouth and was able to pull her out of the flooded creek to safety.

So even though Snores can be mischievous and lazy, he is also a dog of great value. Chores would not give him up for anything in the world.

CHORES AND SNORES
THE MISSING LUNCH

Chores and Snores is a story about two special best friends, a man and his dog.

Chores the man is a carpenter. He spends most of his time painting houses, hammering nails and doing the other things carpenters do.

Snores the dog spends most of his time sleeping. Well . . . most of his time that is.

There are times when even the laziest of dogs have to get up, have something to eat, stretch their legs and run and play.

That is when Snores usually ends up getting himself in trouble. Getting in trouble has always been easy for Snores. Sometimes he just seems to have a nose for it . . .

Like the time he sniffed his way to the sandwiches in Chores' lunch bag. Just as most any other dog would have done, he ate them, leaving nothing behind but crumbs.

Chores was not very happy when he went to have his lunch that day and realized that someone else had already eaten it.

"Where's my lunch?" he shouted. By the looks of things, he had a good idea of who that someone else was.

The lunch bag was lying on the ground torn open and there were crumbs scattered about. Sure enough, that someone else was Snores.

As Chores stood there holding the empty, shredded up lunch bag, he chuckled to himself and said . . . "Looks as though it is time to get myself a lunch box."

And that he did.

CHORES AND SNORES
THE OTHER SIDE OF THE FENCE

It was a beautiful sunny afternoon and Chores decided that it was a good time to get the fence in the backyard painted.

So he put on his painting clothes, got out the paint and brushes, and started painting.

Snores found him a comfortable place in the shade and settled down for a nap.

When Chores had finished with the first side of the fence, he gathered up the paint and brushes and went around to the other side to paint.

Meanwhile, back on the other side of the fence, Snores had become restless and wandered into some bushes nearby. He rustled about within the bushes for a while and suddenly came out carrying an old shoe in his mouth.

Within moments, Snores was running around the yard playing with that old shoe. It was as though he was momentarily reliving his puppyhood.

And that could very well be because that was not just any old shoe, it happened to be the same old shoe that he played with when he was a puppy.

Snores played with the old shoe until he was all

tired out and ready for a nap. But, before settling down to rest, he wanted to bury his old shoe for safekeeping.

He found a good place alongside the fence and started digging. He dug deeper and deeper and as he dug, the freshly painted fence behind him was getting dirtier and dirtier as dirt stuck to the wet paint.

Chores had finished painting the backside of the fence and came around to the other side, just as Snores was finishing up.

He had the old shoe just about buried as Chores looked at the fence and just about screamed. "Oh no!" he shouted, as he walked over to get a closer look at the dirt spattered paint.

Chores could see that Snores had buried something, so he cleared some of the dirt away and pulled out the old shoe. He chuckled as he tossed the shoe over to Snores. "Found your old shoe ha boy", he said.

Chores had to clean and repaint that portion of the fence, but that did not matter to him. He enjoyed watching Snores play around with that old shoe again and he knew that the dirt getting on the fence was just an unfortunate accident. However, it does seem as though Snores dug his way into trouble this time.

But, whatever the cause may be or wherever the place, trouble never has and never will come between Chores and Snores. They will always be the best of friends. Maybe that is what makes them special.

CHORES AND SNORES POEMS

Chores the farmer and his lazy dog Snores poems include topics such as seasonal scenery, holidays, special events, fishing, fruit and vegetable tales, and enjoyable visits from wildlife.

Suitable for all ages

Ann wrote the following poems between 1997 and 2006. They are in the order as written.

AUTUMN WITH CHORES AND SNORES

Chores the farmer and his lazy dog Snores,
jumped into the pickup and set out to find more.
More signs of autumn, the changes and all,
more signs of the season, often called fall.
They went to a park just a few miles away,
a great place to go on a warm autumn's day.
The fall colors were beautiful, so brilliant and bright,
the trees of many colors were an awesome sight.
As Chores admired the colorful trees,
Snores playfully chased the falling leaves.
Squirrels were out scampering around,
gathering acorns that had fell to the ground.
A flock of geese flew overhead,
traveling south for the winter ahead.
Chores and Snores enjoyed being at the park,
but soon it was time for them to depart.
Chores had to get back to work on the farm,
and Snores had to get back to his bed in the barn.
So with Snores beside him asleep on the seat,
Chores started the pickup and drove off down the street.

HALLOWEEN WITH CHORES AND SNORES

Chores the farmer and his lazy dog Snores,
jumped into the pickup and set out to find
more.
More pumpkins that is, perfect for carving,
just the right size, with no major marring.
They went to a place just down the road,
where countless pumpkins are grown and sold.
As Chores looked over various pumpkins,
Snores sat anxiously with his tail a thumpin'.
Chores picked out several that looked just fine,
then carefully cut them away from the vine.
Back at the house, with papers spread onto the
floor,
he started carving the pumpkins, all seven or
more.
Snores watched curiously from his favorite old
chair,
as Chores carved the pumpkins with patience
and care.
A short time later when Snores was asleep,
the carving was over, each jack-o-lantern
complete.
Then with a candle placed inside,
Chores set the jack-o-lanterns on the porch
outside.
There they created an eerie light,
for those who ventured out on Halloween night.

THANKSGIVING WITH CHORES AND SNORES

Chores the farmer and his lazy dog Snores,
have a great deal to be thankful for.
Chores believes that natural things are the most precious,
that thanks should be given for what nature provides for us.
On a farm you work together with nature,
to raise crops that are healthy and mature.
For Thanksgiving dinner Chores was invited out to his brother's farm,
Snores went too since the family thinks he is such a charm.
There was turkey with all the trimmings,
and luscious desserts with various toppings.
Snores waited patiently as everyone ate,
then later was given some scraps on a plate.
He cleaned the plate in no time flat,
then he settled down to take a short nap.
Conversation and laughter filled the house,
outside, the playful children ran about.
Soon it was time for hugs and goodbyes,
Chores was handed a container of leftover pie.
Chores and Snores then headed back to their cozy retreat,
that small old farm along Andrews Street.

A CHRISTMAS TREE FOR CHORES AND SNORES

Chores the farmer and his lazy dog Snores,
needed a Christmas tree to take home and
adorn.
So they got out the ax and the toboggan too,
then went into the woods to find a tree that
would do.
Chores has always been fussy when choosing a
tree,
seeking out any minor flaws that there might be.
He closely examines each tree's shape and size,
allowing nothing to slip by his judging eyes.
When he found the perfect one, he cut it with
the ax,
placed it on the toboggan and then headed
back.
Chores took the tree inside right away,
and started to decorate it for Christmas Day.
As the smell of fresh pine filled the house,
Snores lifted his snout and sniffed about.
When the lights were lit and each ornament was
in place,
it put a wag in Snores' tail and a smile on
Chores' face.
Chores then took a moment to reflect upon the
reason,
the one true reason for the Christmas season.
He later hung two stockings by the chimney with
care,
as Snores slept soundly in his favorite old chair.

CHORES AND SNORES GO FISHING

Chores the farmer and his lazy dog Snores,
got out the boat and got out the oars.
They were going fishing out at the lake,
for supper they would have fisherman's steak.
They fished near the lily pads and cattail reeds,
a place where fish often feed.
Chores wore a life jacket to keep him afloat,
if for some reason he should fall from the boat.
Snores watched a turtle slide off a stump,
then gave his tail a wag and a thump.
When they had their catch, they headed right back,
because poor old Snores needed a nap.
Chores cleaned the fish, then started frying them up,
some for himself and some for that lazy old pup.
Snores relaxed in his favorite old chair,
as the smell of fried fish filled the air.
Chores and Snores enjoyed their fisherman's steak,
it was delicious, well worth the bait.
Chores later went about his work on the farm,
and Snores wandered out to his bed in the barn.

CHORES AND SNORES
WITH SPOOKS AT THE DOOR!

Chores the farmer and his lazy dog Snores,
were really quite frightened by the spooks at
their door.

Some ugly old witches with scraggly hair,
scared Snores so bad that he hid under his chair.

Along with the spooks came eerie sounds too,
there were bone chilling screams and ghostly
boos.

Chores was shaking in his boots after an earful
of that,
he had to get rid of those spooks, no doubt
about that.

Good thing he had that big bowl of candy,
because it sure came in handy.

He gave each spook a chocolaty treat,
then one by one, they ran off down the street.

Hours later, just before dawn,
all was quiet, all the spooks were gone.

Chores and Snores were relieved when it come
daylight,
together they had survived another Halloween
night.

CHORES AND SNORES WITH MANY THANKFULS

Chores the farmer and his lazy dog Snores,
have many things to be thankful for.
Chores is thankful for his chickens and cows,
his pickup truck and his tractors and plows.
He is also thankful for the vast farm fields,
and the crops which they yield.
When he sits down to pray,
he gives thanks for each and every day.
Snores is thankful for his home on the farm,
and even more thankful for his bed in the barn.
He is also thankful for his favorite old chair,
his squeaky toy and the brush for his hair.
When he goes to the vet where he is simply adored,
he wags his tail thankfully as he goes out the door.
Needless to say, Chores is thankful for Snores,
and Snores is thankful for Chores.
On Thanksgiving Day, they will thankfully gobble up some gobbler,
along with some of Mrs. Andrews' homemade cobbler.
Together they will gather with family and friends,
they are thankful for them too, the list never ends.

CHORES AND SNORES BUILD A SNOWMAN

Chores the farmer and his lazy dog Snores,
had never built a snowman together before.

With a new blanket of snow coming down it was
a perfect time,
the snow packed real good and would do just
fine.

Chores took a moment to catch snowflakes on
his tongue,
not that he was hungry; he just did it for fun.

Snores caught snowflakes on the end of his
nose,
then he would take off running and off they
would blow.

Chores made a big snowball, then started
another,
he knew that this snowman would be like no
other.

He soon had three snowballs, each one a
different size,
then he carefully stacked them, putting the
smallest up high.

Chores knew that the snowman needed a hat,
so he rounded up an old milk can lid to use for
that.

He then used tree branches to make the snowman's hands and arms,
and a cob of corn for the nose created a corny kind of charm.

Gumdrops were used to form a sweet smile,
and a corncob pipe to add character and style.

Finally complete with potatoes for his eyes and a pitchfork in his hand,
Chores and Snores then named him Farmer the Snowman.

CHORES, SNORES AND A SNOWASAURUS

Chores the farmer and his lazy dog Snores,
had never seen such a big snowdrift before.
As big as a dinosaur is how big it was,
a snowasaurus is what it was.
Chores is rather tall,
yet the snowasaurus made him look small.
Snores was tiny compared to the large white mass,
yet he tried to climb it and fell on his last.
Right across the driveway is where the snowasaurus sat,
so it had to be moved, no doubt about that.
A snowasaurus cannot move on its own,
it has to be plowed, shoveled, or blown.
Chores worked until he was blue in the face,
moving that snowasaurus to a different place.
He shoveled some snow and plowed some snow,
dug Snores out of the snow and then moved more snow.
Afterwards, Chores had the sniffles and sat blowing his nose,
while Snores pulled ice balls from between his toes.
Chores later went about his work on the farm,
and Snores wandered out to his bed in the barn.

SPRING WITH CHORES AND SNORES

Chores the farmer and his lazy dog Snores,
took a walk in the woods so that they could
explore.
For it was spring and there were changes galore,
much too exciting and much too great to ignore.

Changes could be found all around,
up in the trees and down on the ground.
They were fun to find and were sure to astound,
even for Snores, that lazy old hound.

Robins were cheerfully singing their best,
as they searched for worms to take to their
nests.
The river was high and reaching its crest,
while up on the bank, a mother duck and her
ducklings were getting some rest.

Every plant was in bloom and starting anew,
there were mayflowers, pussy willows and
tadpoles too.
Chores swung at a pesky mosquito or two,
sadly enough, spring brings them too.

They got a glimpse of a mother deer and her
fawn,
but in a moment's time, they had vanished and
gone.
It was right about then that Snores produced a
big yawn,

so Chores thought it was best that they move
right along.

Chores and Snores enjoyed their walk in the
woods that spring day,
there was so much to see along the way.
For it was such a beautiful day,
a beautiful day in the month of May.

CHORES, SNORES AND A TORNADO

Chores the farmer and his lazy dog Snores,
had never encountered a tornado before.

Chores was out in the field doing some plowing,
when the sky grew dark and the wind started
howling.

A heavy rain started coming down,
washing the smile from Chores' face, creating a
frown.

He got down from the tractor and ran for cover,
he knew that storm was like no other.

Snores was nearby and found it all too
frightening,
and took off running as fast as lightning.

Chores called out to him but he just kept going,
where he was headed there was just no
knowing.

Chores laid flat in a ditch with his face in the
clover,
there he stayed until the storm was over.

After the storm, there was scattered debris and
fallen trees,
a heartbreaking sight to see.

Chores searched desperately for poor old

Snores,
he could have been hurt, he could have been
lost, possibilities too great to ignore.

He called out his name and looked all around,
but there was just no sign of that lazy old
hound.

A few of the farm buildings were damaged real
bad,
and that made Chores feel disappointed and
sad.

Yet when he looked up at the sky and seen the
sun shining bright,
he knew that everything was going to be all
right.

Snores was later found sleeping in his bed in the
barn,
soaked to the skin, but safe and unharmed.

Thanks to family and friends who lent a helping
hand,
things were soon back in order and Chores was
out farming the land.

Chores and Snores were fortunate on that
fateful day,
they still have each other and best friends they
will stay.

CHORES, SNORES AND A GREAT BIG JACK-O-LANTERN

Chores the farmer and his lazy dog Snores,
grew a pumpkin that was bigger than any before.

It was a giant and weighed hundreds of pounds,
so Chores had to roll it to move it around.

He grunted and groaned, pushed and rolled,
moving the pumpkin over crisp autumn leaves of yellow and gold.

After the pumpkin was carved, Snores jumped inside,
perhaps to take a nap, or maybe just to hide.

Whatever the reason it did not work out,
it was cold and damp in there, so he jumped back out.

Chores saved some of the seeds for next year's crop,
and used the rest of the innards to feed the livestock.

The smell of pumpkin seemed to follow Snores everywhere; he kept getting occasional whiffs,
he finally realized that the smell had gotten into his hair after giving himself a couple of sniffs.

Chores later prepared a bowl of Halloween treats,
putting several aside for himself to eat.

Snores settled down for a nap in his favorite old chair,
it was warm and dry in there and it would not leave a smell in his hair.

Trick-or-treaters were amazed at the jack-o-lantern's size,
they stood and studied it with judging eyes.

They described it as being big,
huge, enormous, gigantic and great big!

It was both fascinating and frightening to see,
such a big carved out face looking eerie as could be.

Chores and Snores had a great Halloween night,
with their great big jack-o-lantern shining so bright.

CHORES, SNORES AND A CALF NAMED MILLENNIUM

Chores the farmer and his lazy dog Snores,
had a New Year's Eve unlike any before.
Snores was fast asleep in his bed in the barn,
when he was awakened by a sound, which was
cause for alarm.
Betsy, the cow, had gone into labor,
but she was in distress as things were not in her
favor.
Snores stretched his legs and produced a big
yawn,
then set out into the dark wee hours just before
dawn.
Chores was fast asleep too, but had to be
awakened,
Betsy needed his help there was no mistaken.
Snores stood outside the house and barked and
yelped,
he had to wake Chores, he had to get help.
The calf was breech so Chores turned it around,
then it was delivered and placed beside Betsy,
safe and sound.
Since the year 2000 had just begun,
Chores named the calf Millennium, just for fun.
Snores would be rewarded, no doubt about
that,
he started to doze off though, so first he needed
a nap.
Chores and Snores both fell asleep in the barn
that day,
they slept there peacefully atop the hay.

STRINGING POPCORN WITH CHORES AND SNORES

Chores the farmer and his lazy dog Snores,
jumped into the pickup and went to the store.

Chores was going to trim the Christmas tree
with popcorn on a string,
so he had to buy popcorn, cooking oil, a needle,
and of course, some string.

Snores was exhausted when they arrived back
home,
so he climbed into his favorite old chair with a
grunt and a groan.

Chores popped the corn the old-fashioned way,
in a kettle atop the stove instead of using a
popper or microwave.

Snores was awakened by the popping corn,
he had not heard or smelt anything like it since
the day he was born.

He perked his ears and lifted his snout,
what was that noise and that smell all about?

Why would food be so noisy to make,
why not fry it, boil it, or bake?

Chores raised his brow and widened his eyes,
when the lid on the kettle started to rise.

page 2 / Stringing Popcorn

He had used too much popcorn, no doubt about that,
popped kernels spilled from the kettle, falling this way and that.

Chores spent hours stringing popcorn and eating it too,
Snores even ate a kernel or two.

Chores and Snores had a popcorn filled Christmas that year,
together they rekindled some of that old-fashioned holiday cheer.

PLAYING IN THE SNOW WITH CHORES AND SNORES

Chores the farmer and his lazy dog Snores,
played in the snow like never before.
The snow was long overdue and brought great joy,
causing Snores to feel like a pup and Chores to feel like a boy.
Chores made a snow-angel, then another and another,
Snores even made a snow-something or other.
Chores threw snowballs for Snores to chase,
but poor old Snores just could not keep pace.
Chasing those snowballs was too much for him,
he tried and tried again, but he just could not win.
Chores caught snowflakes on the end of his tongue,
he looked ridiculous, but it sure was fun.
They went inside when they were all played out,
Chores had a cold nose and Snores a cold snout.
After pulling the ice balls from between his toes,
Snores climbed into his favorite old chair and started to doze.
Chores sipped on hot chocolate and sat by the fire,
a bit too close though, as he started to perspire.
Chores and Snores enjoyed playing in the snow that day,
come spring, it will all melt away.

A NEW TRUCK FOR CHORES AND SNORES

Chores the farmer and his lazy dog Snores,
came to the conclusion their old pickup truck
was not fit anymore.
The old clunker had seen its better days,
and was starting to fail in various ways.
It knocked, shimmied and sputtered about,
it guzzled gas and was all rusted out.
They needed a new truck, no doubt about that,
perhaps a red one, blue, white, or black.
Chores is quite fussy yet a used one would do,
if it were in mint condition and the price was
right too.
So they went truck shopping and it did not take
long,
they had soon found the perfect one and they
could not go wrong.
It was just like new, all shiny and white,
with modern features and fancy taillights.
Chores kicked the tires and looked under the
hood,
took it for a test drive and all checked out good.
Snores jumped in and sprawled out on the seat,
while Chores tried out the radio, air conditioning
and heat.
They ride with pride in their new pickup truck,
just as they did in their old pickup truck.

CHORES, SNORES AND APPLES GALORE

Chores the farmer and his lazy dog Snores,
ended up with apples, apples galore.
They had went to the market to buy a bushel,
not more,
but the price was too good for Chores to ignore.
So he bought two bushels, then he bought two
more,
he kept buying apples until he could not buy any
more.
He had bought them all, the market had no
more,
and his pickup truck could not hold any more.
Chores later peeled apples until his fingers were
sore,
he peeled until he just could not peel anymore.
He was up to his elbows in apple cores,
and peelings were piled high on the kitchen
table and floor.
There were peelings stuck to the apron he wore,
and there were peelings stuck to poor old
Snores.
Snores had been sniffing around in the peelings
and cores,
when he fell asleep there on the floor.
Chores made apple pies like never before,
he would make some and bake some, then
make some more.
He made at least three dozen or more,
he made apple pies, apple pies galore.
Snores had never tasted apple pie before,

yet the smell of those pies he just could not ignore.
So he reached onto the table and pulled one to the floor,
he devoured it quickly and then had one more.
Chores was surprised when he found two empty pie tins there on the floor,
because Snores had never eaten apple pie before.
Yet there were crumbs in the tins and crumbs on the floor,
sure enough, those pies had been eaten by Snores.
When the rest of the pies were cooled off and ready to store,
Chores put them in the freezer, all thirty-four.
He also made candy apples, applesauce and much, much more,
and he gave some apples to his neighbors next door.
Chores and Snores enjoyed having apples galore,
but next time they will buy just a bushel, not more.

EASTER WITH CHORES AND SNORES

Chores the farmer and his lazy dog Snores,
wanted to celebrate Easter like never before.
So they jumped into the pickup and went to the store,
they bought a basket, egg coloring and much, much more.

They also bought two stuffed rabbits, one pink and one blue,
some Easter grass and jelly beans, a ham and dog bones too.
They also wanted something that would smell refreshing and new,
so they stopped by the florist and bought an Easter lily too.

Snores was exhausted when they arrived back home,
so he craved for a nap instead of a bone.
He climbed from the pickup with a grunt and a groan,
then climbed into his favorite old chair with a relaxing kind of moan.

Chores gathered eggs from the chicken coop,
then he carefully washed them on the back stoop.
One of the eggs fell from his hands and smashed on his boot,
yet he remained calm and just said, "Whoops."

After the eggs were boiled he colored them one by one,
there were many eggs of many colors when he was done.
He then placed the eggs into the basket one by one,
he was feeling mighty hungry though, so he ate just one.

It was soon Easter Sunday,
and it was a beautiful day.
The countryside glistened beneath the sun's warm, bright rays,
and birds were singing in a harmonious way.

Chores and Snores took a leisurely walk as part of their holiday treat,
it was great except for the little hill that Snores thought was too steep.
For lunch, Chores had boiled eggs and ham to eat,
and Snores had dog bones and ham, then fell right to sleep.

CHORES, SNORES AND A WREATH FOR THEIR DOOR

Chores the farmer and his lazy dog Snores,
wanted a wreath to hang on their door.

So they got out the sled and went into the woods,
they gathered branches and pinecones as fast as they could.

A heavy snow had started to come down,
covering everything in sight for miles around.

Chores pulled the sled behind him and Snores walked alongside,
until Snores became tired and decided to ride.

He climbed onto the sled with a grunt and a groan,
there he rode with the branches and pinecones.

They were covered with snow when they got back to the farm,
so they cleaned themselves off and then put the sled in the barn.

They were extremely cold and feeling frozy,
so they rushed into the house where it was warm and cozy.

Snores climbed into his favorite old chair,
and fell asleep without a moment to spare.

The poor old pup was totally exhausted,
and needed to have his paws defrosted.

Chores made the wreath without delay,
because there was not much time before
Christmas Day.

He worked with determination and kept a good
pace,
and soon had all the branches and pinecones in
place.

He then added a string of Christmas lights,
so the wreath could shine bright throughout the
night.

Up on the top he put a big red bow,
and down on the bottom he put a big green
bow.

The wreath was then complete and it was
beautiful too,
why it was so beautiful, it made the cows moo!

Chores and Snores were proud of the wreath for
their door,
and because they made it themselves, it made
them proud all the more.

SPRING-CLEANING WITH CHORES AND SNORES

Chores the farmer and his lazy dog Snores,
washed the windows and mopped the floors.

They cleaned the stove and the refrigerator too,
sorted through clothes and threw out old shoes.

Except for the ones that Snores decided to keep,
he hid them in a place where Chores would not
peek.

They shook out the rugs and vacuumed the
drapes,
cleaned the pantry and polished the plates.

They dusted off the mantel and cleaned the
clock,
sorted through boots and threw out old socks.

Except for the ones that Snores decided to keep,
he hid them in a place where Chores would not
peek.

They wiped away cobwebs and swept up dust
bunnies,
bundled up newspapers and reread the funnies.

They put away the coats and hung jackets on
the racks,
sorted through gloves and threw out old hats.

*Except for the ones that Snores decided to keep,
he hid them in a place where Chores would not
peek.*

*By the end of the day the spring-cleaning was
done,
it was a lot of work and a lot of fun.*

*The old farmhouse was spotless and clean,
even the woodstove sparkled and gleamed.*

*Chores was quite tired but had to tend to the
cows,
so he would get some sleep later when time
would allow.*

*Snores was totally exhausted, needless to say,
so he had to get some sleep without delay.*

*He fell fast asleep in his favorite old chair,
and he had more than one reason to fall asleep
there.*

*He had found many treasures throughout the
course of the day,
and there beneath his chair is where he had
them all hidden away.*

*He had three old shoes, two old boots, a musty
old hat, an old pair of socks and a tattered
old glove,*

the kinds of things that most dogs love.

So he was not just sleeping in his favorite old
chair, he was also guarding his stash,
because if Chores found it he would throw it all
right back in the trash.

But the funny thing is . . . Chores already knew
about it,
and he was going to let Snores keep all of it.

Chores knows that those kinds of things make
great dog toys,
and he was not about to deprive Snores of such
great joy.

They say that one man's trash is the next man's
treasure,
what one throws out may bring another
pleasure.

Chores and Snores enjoyed doing spring-
cleaning,
although Snores gave the term a somewhat
different meaning.

They will do it all again come next spring,
and only time will tell what treasures it will
bring.

CHORES AND SNORES GO ICE FISHING

*Chores the farmer and his lazy dog Snores,
got out the tip-ups and much, much more.*

*They were going ice fishing out at the lake,
for supper they would have fisherman's steak.*

*So they loaded up the pickup and set out for the day,
they stopped by the bait shop and bought minnows on the way.*

*Chores used an auger to drill holes in the ice,
he made three holes, three was suffice.*

*Snores went along behind and drank from each hole,
totally unaware of the fish down below.*

*The water was so cold it made him shiver,
and when a fish nipped at his nose, it made him quiver.*

*Chores baited the hooks, then put the tip-ups in place,
he had that hungry-for-fish look on his face.*

*They soon had a bite and up went a flag,
causing Snores to give his tail a couple of wags.*

Chores went running with Snores trailing behind,

both anxious to find what was tugging on their
line.

It was a fish and it was a big one too,
no doubt about it, that one would do.

But within moments, they had another bite,
another big catch, a fisherman's delight.

That was enough fish for them and Snores
needed a nap,
so they loaded up the pickup and headed back.

Chores cleaned the fish, then fried them up,
some for himself and some for that lazy old pup.

Snores relaxed in his favorite old chair,
as the smell of fried fish filled the air.

Chores and Snores enjoyed their fisherman's
steak,
it was delicious, well worth the bait.

Chores later went about his work on the farm,
and Snores wandered out to his bed in the barn.

CHORES, SNORES AND DANDELIONS GALORE

Chores the farmer and his lazy dog Snores,
had more dandelions in their yard than ever
before.
There were hundreds, thousands, maybe more,
there were countless dandelions, there were
dandelions galore.

They were everywhere possible from the house
to the barn,
making the place look like a dandelion farm.
Chores did not mind, he knew they were no
harm,
he was actually delighted by all the country
charm.

The wildflowers were a beautiful sight,
like miniature suns, colored yellow so bright.
Like most flowers they would close at night,
then open again come daylight.

Snores did not care if the dandelions were
yellow or red,
because he did not think they were pretty, he
thought they were useful instead.
They were soft, fluffy and made great beds,
so he had many comfy places to rest his head.

Chores used dandelion leaves to make things to
eat,
such as boiled greens for a tasty treat.

Dandelion leaf salads just cannot be beat,
and they would make most any meal complete.

A local photographer came around,
and took some pictures of the dandelion
covered grounds.
He also took a picture of that lazy old hound,
laying there among the dandelions, sleeping so
sound.

Chores and Snores enjoyed having dandelions
galore,
their usefulness and beauty were just too great
to ignore.
Perhaps next year there will be even more,
providing more salads for Chores and more
flowerbeds for Snores.

CHORES, SNORES AND THE BIGGEST COB OF CORN

Chores the farmer and his lazy dog Snores,
grew a cob of corn bigger than any before.
Chores could hardly believe his eyes,
that cob of corn was enormous in size.
In all his years of farming, he had never seen anything like it,
he knew that it would be the biggest cob of corn he would ever pick.
It was ready for picking and it was sweet corn too,
so Chores knew exactly what to do.
He carefully picked that big cob of corn,
making sure nothing got broken and nothing got torn.
Then he took some pictures and then he took some measurements,
he was all caught up in all the excitement.
It was a world record, no doubt about that,
so he needed those pictures and measurements to prove that fact.
Chores became hungry, as it was then time for lunch,
the menu was corn on the cob, a lot, a bunch.
But the corn had to be cleaned before it could be cooked,
and it would take a little time by the way it looked.
Chores removed the husk piece by piece, tossing it into a pile,
Snores watched patiently all the while.

Chores then removed the big tassel and tossed that into the pile as well,
the silky green strands danced through the air, and then gently fell.
Then he searched through the cupboards to find the biggest kettle,
the biggest was not big enough, but for that he would settle.
He had to break the cob of corn into several pieces to fit it all in,
then he put in the water and let the cooking begin.
That corn smelled so good cooking in the pot,
it even had Snores licking his chops.
When the corn was done cooking and ready to eat,
Chores added a lot of butter and some salt and pepper to make it complete.
Those big yellow kernels looked so tasty and delicious,
why they could make a hungry man vicious!
Chores started to eat without delay,
he ate the corn right off the cob, the usual way.
By the time he was done eating he had corn on his mustache and corn on his chin,
and neither his lap nor the floor was as neat as a pin.
He did not mind the mess for he had had himself a feast,
a feast of some of the finest corn in the world, to say the very least.

Snores climbed onto the pile of the soft cornhusk,
all that excitement had made him extremely tired; a good nap was a must!
He fell fast asleep on his cornhusk bed,
he knew that it would be a comfy place to rest his head.
Chores patted his belly and fell asleep in the chair,
there among the big kernels of corn, they were everywhere!
Chores and Snores enjoyed having the biggest cob of corn,
it was so exciting it left them both tired and worn.

GOBBLING UP TURKEY WITH CHORES AND SNORES

Chores the farmer and his lazy dog Snores,
gobbled up some turkey and much, much more.

They also had mashed potatoes and gravy,
dressing and yams,
cranberries, corn and ham.

Fresh bread, neatly sliced,
with creamy butter that spread on nice.

Carrot sticks and celery sticks,
with a delicious homemade dip.

For dessert they had pumpkin pie with whipped
topping,
though such an abundance of food made it
seem like there was no stopping.

Chores used the wishbone to wish for world
peace,
for the wars to end, for fighting to cease.

Chores and Snores are thankful for many things,
but mostly they are thankful for family, friends,
and the joy that they bring.

CHORES AND SNORES
GO TO AN EASTER EGG HUNT

Chores the farmer and his lazy dog Snores,
had never been to an Easter egg hunt before.

So they were very excited when they received
an invitation to one,
there would be many eggs to hunt for, exactly
two hundred and one.

The egg hunt was for everyone, children and
adults alike,
it would be festive and fun, a sure delight!

The Easter egg hunt was held on a nearby farm,
eggs were hidden from the house to the barn.

By the silos and windmill, by the tractors and
plow,
most anywhere, that would allow.

The eggs were made of plastic and were various
colors and sizes,
each egg was numbered and they all contained
prizes.

Except for egg number two hundred and one,
that held a ticket for the grand prize,
which was a stuffed Easter rabbit, jumbo size!

Each participant was given a bag, then at the
sound of a whistle the egg hunt began,

in every direction the anxious egg hunters ran.

Some had a big smile on their face,
others looked determined and kept a steady
pace.

Hunting for eggs brought out the child in
Chores,
he had a smile on his face too big to ignore.

Whenever he found an egg, he would shout out
the word "Yes!"
then drop it into his bag with the rest.

Snores settled down in a sunny spot near a big
oak tree,
since it was a cool spring day of only 50 degrees.

The sun's warm rays felt good, no doubt about
that,
a great place indeed for him to take a good nap.

Most of the eggs had soon been found all except
for one,
that one egg yet to be found was egg number
two hundred and one.

Everyone was curious and looking around
wondering where that egg could be,
when suddenly they all heard a funny sound
coming from near the big oak tree.

Snores was there rustling around in the dry
leaves and came out grasping the egg in his
mouth,
he ran up to Chores with his tail wagging and
Chores took the egg from his mouth.

Everyone cheered and applauded for the
missing egg had been found,
but whoever thought that it would be found by
Snores, Snores that lazy old hound!

CHORES, SNORES AND ROOSTER CROW

Chores the farmer and his lazy dog Snores,
met a rooster that can crow like none before.

Where he came from they do not know,
but one thing for certain, that rooster can crow!

He starts to crow at the break of dawn,
starting at the hen house, then making his way
across the lawn.

He wakes up Chores, Snores and their
neighbors too,
with his extremely loud cock-a-doodle-doos!

He struts with dignity; no doubt he is proud,
he knows that he crows extremely loud.

He is quite a handsome fellow,
with silky black feathers and a big red comb that
jiggles like Jell-O.

He has a job to do and he does it well,
when he will retire only time will tell.

Chores and Snores have become fond of the
rooster despite his extremely loud crows,
so they have made him a part of the family and
named him Rooster Crow!

CHORES, SNORES AND A GIANT TOMATO PLANT

Chores the farmer and his lazy dog Snores,
grew a tomato plant that was bigger than any before.

Chores could hardly believe his eyes,
that tomato plant was enormous in size!

It was a giant, no doubt about that,
thirteen feet tall as a matter of fact.

If there was such a thing as a tomato tree,
no doubt about it that is what it would be.

It had many branches and was tall and strong,
which allowed songbirds to rest there and sing their songs.

Chores had to use a stepladder to reach up to the top,
he picked ripe tomatoes from there and there were a lot.

He picked from the middle and the bottom too,
there were a lot of ripe tomatoes in those places too.

The very next day there would be even more,
more ripe tomatoes, tomatoes galore!

Chores used tomatoes in chili, sandwiches,

salads and such,
but one man can only eat so much.

So he sold tomatoes by the dozen and by the
pound,
people came to buy them from miles around.

He gave tomatoes to his neighbors and friends,
until the harvest season came to an end.

Snores found a use for the giant tomato plant
too,
the shade that it produced made a great place
for him to snooze.

He took a snooze beside the giant tomato plant
most every day, until a ripe tomato fell and
hit him atop the head,
he then returned to one of his usual places to
snooze and rest his tired, then with a goose-
egg head.

Chores and Snores enjoyed having a giant
tomato plant,
they both found it to be useful and the
experience was really quite pleasant.

CHORES, SNORES AND COOKIE DOE

Chores the farmer and his lazy dog Snores,
had never made friends with a deer before.

But they did just that one spring day,
when a hungry doe wandered their way.

Chores was busy baking cookies,
and decorating them with all kinds of goodies.

He had opened a kitchen window just a crack,
to help cool the hot cookies that he had placed on the rack.

Those freshly baked cookies smelled so good,
they caused a hungry deer to wander out of the woods.

The deer was so hungry she followed that smell right up to the porch,
where she tapped a hoof and let out a snort!

Snores, whom had been asleep, sprung from his bed,
he raised his ears and turned his head.

He knew there was someone outside the door,
but no one had ever knocked like that before.

Chores was quite concerned too,
so he took a peek out the window, which was the safest thing to do.

When he looked out the window he seen a thin
white-tailed doe,
what a wild deer was doing on his porch he did
not know.

But he did know that something had to be
wrong,
because there on his porch a wild deer just did
not belong!

The doe kept lifting her snout and smelling the
air,
and that is what made Chores become suddenly
aware.

The doe was starving and had to eat,
so he tossed her a couple of cookies to eat.

She ate them hastily, so he tossed her one
more,
then another, then one more.

The doe then nodded her head with gratitude
and went on her way,
though she still returns for another cookie or
two every few days.

Sometimes she will frolic and play with Snores
there on the lawn,
in the early evening, or just after dawn.

page 3 / Cookie Doe

Chores enjoys watching them,
he has not seen anything like it since he does not know when.

Chores and Snores have made a dear, deer friend,
and that is how they will stay right up to the end.

They decided to name her Cookie Doe,
after all, the name does fit you know.

CAT POEMS

Ann was an animal lover. She had a special place in her heart for cats. Therefore, I decided to put her cat poems in a special place all their own.

Suitable for all ages

Ann wrote the following poems between 1995 and 1999.

AFTER DINNER CAT

After a hearty meal of Chicken of the Sea,
I am ready for a good long nap you see.

But first, I have to pause,
to lick and clean my paws.

And wash and wipe my nose,
just a common routine any cat knows.

Then I primp and shine my tail,
and prepare to dream a feline tale.

As I lay my tired body down,
on a soft fluffy pillow of down.

I LIKE TO HAVE A CAT

I like to have a cat on my lap
when I watch television.
The cat takes a nap,
the cat takes a nap on my lap.

I like to have a cat in my bed
when I go to sleep.
The cat steps on my head,
the cat steps on my head in my bed.

I like to have a cat in my house
when I have a mouse in my house.
The cat catches the mouse,
the cat catches the mouse in my house.

I like to have a cat in my yard
when I go outside.
The cat runs from afar,
the cat runs from afar in my yard.

I like to have a cat for my friend
because I never get lonely.
And the friendship will never end,
the cat will always be by friend.

THESE BEST FRIENDS OF MINE

These best friends of mine,
my beautiful, precious felines.

They make my house seem more like a home,
and fill it with a special warmth of their own.

They take away my loneliness,
and replace it with true happiness.

They comfort me during the bad times,
and put more joy into the good times.

They make the dark days bright,
and are there at my side throughout the dark nights.

They make me laugh and smile,
and make my life more worthwhile.

They are entertaining and playful,
and my love for them is never doubtful.

They mean the world to me you see,
and the best of friends we will always be.

These best friends of mine,
my beautiful, precious felines.

CITY CAT

City cat sits in the window ever so proud,
as she watches the hustle and bustle crowd.
She observes the cars of many shapes and colors,
and notices how different each looks from the others.
She hears the roaring of engines and the honking of horns,
and wonders what all those loud noises are for.
She watches pedestrians pass by as they pound the pavement beneath their feet,
and take great strides as they rush across the busy city streets.
Suddenly she sees a familiar face in the crowd,
and jumps down from the window with a leap and a bound.
Her owner has returned home from the grocery store,
and has brought back some cat food and much, much more!
She is soon given a serving of her favorite food,
and a fresh platter of milk is set out for her too.
She cleans her plate without fail,
and then washes herself thoroughly from head to tail.
Then she jumps up onto her owner's lap,
and settles down to take a short nap.
All the commotion outside is no concern to her now,
but perhaps someday she will understand it somehow.

A DOZEN KITTENS

A dozen kittens all fluffy and spry,
chasing about a butterfly.
They chase one another and chase their own tails,
and will chase the wind when all else fails.
They pause briefly for a morsel of food, just a nibble, a bite,
and a few laps of milk if only they might.
With curious eyes they look all around,
and will perk their ears at even the slightest of sounds.
They like to play with their kitty cat toys,
yet a falling leaf can bring them great joy.
If you give them a kiss,
they may feel threatened and give you a hiss.
Soon they are tired and need a good nap,
but they must lick themselves clean prior to that.
With the kittens all nestled and purring so loud,
the ma cat looks on ever so proud.
Twelve months later, a dozen that is,
the kittens have grown, a dozen cats there now is.
A dozen cats all fully grown,
soon they will have kittens of their own.

VARIOUS TOPICS POEMS

The following poems include topics such as seasonal beauty, wildlife, road construction, holidays, special memories, the circus, clowns, Wisconsin, school, special people, silly critters, teddy bears, the Peanuts gang, and America.

Suitable for all ages

Ann wrote the following poems between 1995 and 2011. They are in the order as written.

THE AUTUMN LEAVES

One by one the autumn leaves break free,
then gently fall away from the tree.

They tumble about on their way down,
then settle softly upon the ground.

There together they lay at rest,
after giving the summer their very best.

Then a sudden brisk wind sets them in motion,
they move around hastily in a dance of
commotion.

There is a renewed calm when the wind dies
down,
once again, the leaves settle softly upon the
ground.

It is there together they lay at rest,
after giving the summer their very best.

MEMORY BOUQUET

I took a walk in the woods one spring day,
I picked some wildflowers along the way.

I had soon picked a fistful,
a bouquet that was most beautiful.

The flower's petals were bright and radiant,
the leafy green stems long and elegant.

Yet there was much more beauty there in the
woods,
I could see it and hear it from where I stood.

There were towering trees all around,
velvety moss and ferns covered much of the
ground.

Throughout the woods birds were singing,
in a nearby pond, frogs were croaking.

Volumes were spoken by a gentle breeze,
its soft voice whispered through the tops of the
trees.

I got a glimpse of a mother deer and her fawn,
but in a moment's time, they had vanished and
gone.

I will never forget my walk in the woods that
spring day,
I will always remember my memory bouquet.

HOMELESS PETS

Left without a home
in this world all alone.

They long to be loved
just like everyone does.

They need someone who really cares
and has some time to share.

Someone to adopt them as their own
and will come to take them home.

THE 8th STREET CONSTRUCTION

Road Closed signs and barricades are a common sight these days,
the 8th Street construction is now underway.

A section of road once highly traveled,
now lays unpaved, dug up and unraveled.

Observers look on from various places,
mixed expressions displayed on their faces.

Motorists scurry around in search of their destinations,
as they make their way through the detours and all the traffic congestion.

Sounds of heavy machinery are heard throughout the construction site,
followed by a peaceful calm brought on by each day's night.

The times are changing and so must our street,
more traffic to handle and new standards to meet.

The 8th Street construction will be done soon,
the street will then be much safer and easier to travel too.

THE 4th OF JULY

The 4th of July,
Independence Day.
When the dark night sky
lights up with a fireworks display,
as we celebrate our freedom
in the traditional way.
May it bring us all good reason
to stand right up and say . . .
"We are proud to be Americans,
God bless the USA."

THE OLD FARM

There was an old farm where I used to go,
and visit relatives some years ago.
A rusty old windmill stood quiet and still,
until the wind moved its sails, creating a
squeaky shrill.
The floors moaned and creaked in the old
house,
it allowed no one to walk quietly except for a
mouse.
Milk house cats peeped through the tall grass,
they awaited fresh milk to remedy their thirst at
last.
Grandma's kisses, so precious and sweet,
given by the kitchen door just as we would
meet.
There were cornfields, pastures and Holstein
cows,
a barn and silos, tractors and plows.
Callused and weathered were the farmer's
hands,
due to many years of working the land.
Outside near the barn pigeons would coo,
at night near the house, a white owl would
hoot.
The place was like a natural treasure,
filled with precious moments, adventure and
pleasure.
Fond memories are worth more than gold,
like the ones of the old farm, I so dearly hold.

HALLOWEEN NIGHT

On Halloween night there is so much to do,
there are costume parties and spook houses
too.
Along with the bone chilling screams and
ghostly boos,
there are caramel apples, cookies and other
good food.

With autumn leaves rustling beneath their feet,
little ones in costumes take to the street.
They go door to door and yell, "Trick or Treat!"
they fill their bags with candy to eat.

Jack-o-lanterns of all sizes are seen everywhere,
their fancy faces carved with the utmost care.
Pranksters just seem to jump out of nowhere,
they wear creepy looking masks with scraggly
hair.

Wicked witches with pointed black hats,
goblins and ghosts, phantoms and bats.
They will be out there, no doubt about that,
lurking around until daylight comes back.

As you venture out on Halloween night,
be prepared for all the scares and frights.
You are sure to encounter some spooky sights,
along with all the things that go bump in the
night.

CONSTRUCTION PAPER TURKEYS

Made by little children with Thanksgiving Day in mind,
the construction paper turkeys are created with pride.
Each one is a little different, a truly rare find,
yet closely resembles all the others of its kind.
Pieces are cut from festive colored paper,
then they are fastened together with glue or a stapler.
A few minor details can be added later,
perhaps a hint of body texture will give the work more stature.
In order to make their head complete,
each turkey is given a yellow beak.
Some other things they are sure to need,
are two yellow legs and two yellow feet.
On the front of their neck, there is a red dewlap,
it creates a dignified look that all turkeys have.
Some may be wearing a pilgrim's top hat,
a traditional symbol of Thanksgiving's past.
Finally, the tail feathers are put in place,
this enhances the turkey's natural grace.
A warm glow appears on each child's face,
as their turkey is then displayed in its own special space.
These works of art with such fine design,
express great respect for this grateful time.
The construction paper turkeys created with pride,
made by little children with Thanksgiving Day in mind.

EIGHT SOGGY RAINDEER

Santa was busy preparing the sleigh and feeding his deer,
it was late December and Christmas Eve was drawing near.
He needed to pack some extra supplies that year,
for a drastic change in the weather was also drawing near.

An oncoming heat wave was in the forecast,
due to bring about a major thaw extremely fast.
Within hours, the winter scenery was becoming past,
even the strongest of snowmen would not last.

The snow had soon melted and the rooftops were bare,
there was not a single flake of snow left anywhere.
The sudden change in weather caused the children no despair,
they knew that Santa Claus would still be there.

Soon a heavy rain started coming down,
down on the villages and down on the towns.
So Santa and his raindeer made their rounds,
up on the housetops there came a different sound.

The raindeer's hooves went clippity clop, clippity clop,

as they scampered upon the bare rooftops.
Through Christmas Eve night they worked
nonstop,
then they headed back to the North Pole after
the last stop.

Santa Claus then did his famous raindeer call,
"On Splasher, on Splatter, on Showers and
Rainy.
On Downpour and Drizzle, Sprinkles and Misty,
now splash away, splash away, splash away all!"

VALENTINE KINDS

Words of love written in rhyme,
printed on a card called a Valentine.

A heart shaped box decorated so fine,
filled with candy of various kinds.

A beautiful bouquet made with fragrant flowers,
put in a vase to be cherished for hours.

A gift wrapped in paper of festive colors,
with a name card addressed to a significant
other.

A prominent single red rose,
its graceful beauty displayed just so.

A plush teddy bear with its warm face aglow,
nicely adorned with a bright red bow.

A candlelight dinner for two,
perhaps there will be a little dancing too.

Cards made with crayons, paper and glue,
made for their parents by children at school.

Breakfast in bed, served on a tray,
a call from a loved one from far away.

Loving feelings expressed in such special ways,
on that special day called Saint Valentine's Day.

THE CIRCUS SHOW

Whenever the circus comes to town,
people tend to gather from miles around.

There are courageous acts by acrobats,
spectacular performances by very large cats.

The magnificent elephants are so enormous in
size,
they are sure to amaze you and open your eyes.

There are trained birds, horses and dogs to see,
a couple of playful monkeys and a high trapeze.

Laughter and smiles are always abound,
during comical stunts by the circus clowns.

You can enjoy soda pop, hot dogs and other fun
foods,
such as fresh roasted popcorn and cotton candy
too!

So if you are looking for excitement and a great
place to go,
go to the circus, the traveling show.

IF I WERE A CLOWN

If I were a clown,
I would wear funny clothes.
I would juggle and dance,
and have a red nose.

If I were a clown,
I would blow up balloons . . .
shape them like animals,
and wear funny shoes.

If I were a clown,
I would change frowns into smiles.
I would be with a circus,
and travel miles and miles.

If I were a clown,
I would have a horn that goes beep.
I would be in parades,
and do tricks in the streets.

If I were a clown,
I would have a funny name . . .
like Zippers or Giggles,
and gain fortune and fame.

That is what I would do,
if I were a clown.
I would be the best clown too,
the best clown around.

*THE WISCONSIN STATE WATER SKI SHOW TOURNAMENT**

Held annually at Lake Wazeecha's Red Sand Beach,
a beautiful rustic location that is sure to please.
This grand event is so very exciting to see,
there is such great entertainment performed on skis.
Numerous ski teams will take turns performing,
as a panel of judges observe and do scoring.
You will see a variety of skiing as the teams perform,
you will see pyramids, freestyle, jumping, ballet lines and more.
There are comedy acts to add a touch of humor to the show,
because a little clowning around is always good you know.
Do not worry about lunch; there will be plenty to eat,
served right there, out at the beach.
So put on your sunglasses and head on out,
you will have a splashing great time without a doubt!

**The Wisconsin State Water Ski Show Tournament is every July in Wisconsin Rapids, Wisconsin.*

BACK TO SCHOOL NEWS

When it is time to head back to school,
there is so much to get and so much is new.

Crayons, paper, pencils and glue,
a nifty backpack and a new pair of shoes.

A haircut or trim, a new style or do,
a new pair of jeans made of denim so blue.

A lunch box and thermos so shiny and new,
a new pair of scissors and a folder or two.

There will be a new desk and a new classroom
too,
new books to read and a new locker to use.

There will be classmates, some old and some
new,
there will be a new teacher too.

There will be new lessons to learn and new
homework to do,
learning is fun and school is fun too!

THE WISCONSIN RAPIDS STORY

There were once two small towns,
with a river running through.
There was a west side town,
and an east side town too.

The west side town was called Centralia,
the east side town was called Grand Rapids.
In 1900, a merger united Grand Rapids and Centralia,
which resulted in one town called Wisconsin Rapids.

A single wooden bridge spanned across the river then,
creating a passageway from shore to shore.
The wooden bridge was narrow but quite suitable then,
when the main means of travel was on foot or by horse.

Today the main means of travel is the automobile,
the streets that were once dirt are now paved.
There have been many changes with notable appeal,
since the town has grown and developed in so many ways.

Three bridges span across the river now,
all made with modern materials and built real good.

page 2 / The Wisconsin Rapids Story

Yet the Grand Avenue Bridge seems special somehow,
standing so boldly, where the town's first bridge once stood.

The town's descriptive nickname, which is River Cities,
is a nickname really quite well known.
As for the local residents of the Wisconsin Rapids city,
it is also a place called home.

*TRIBUTE TO HOWARD**

Clear or cloudy, rain or snow,
whatever kind of weather was coming our way.
Howard Gernetzke would let us know,
when he gave the forecast for the upcoming
day.

Out on the weather deck he would sometimes
be,
always dressed accordingly in a jacket or
shirtsleeves.
He would mention pretty scenery that was there
to see,
when he would give the weather forecast from
outside by the trees.

Through years of dedication and great style,
he became a popular and much admired
weatherman.
He could brighten your day with his warm sunny
smile,
he always kept weather updates close at hand.

Whatever the forecast may the sun always
shine,
in memory of a man, so honored and so kind.

**Howard Gernetzke was a weatherman for WSAW-TV in Wausau, Wisconsin. He passed away on February 6, 1998.*

THE LILAC BUSH

In the spring of the year,
as summer draws near.

The lilac bush goes into full bloom,
creating an abundance of beauty for all eyes to
consume.

There are large clusters of little flowers,
consisting of pale purple, pink, or white colors.

With a distinguished fragrance of their very
own,
the lilac scent for which they are known.

A place where many fine songs are heard,
sung ever so proudly by various birds.

Where the bees are as busy as they can be,
pollinating all the little flowers they see.

A haven for squirrels, rabbits and such,
providing the refuge, they need so much.

Lilacs make great bouquets,
they can freshen your home and brighten your
day.

The lilac bush is not only beautiful,
it is also quite bountiful.

DUCK WATCHING

It is fun to sit and watch the ducks,
as they swim about the bay.
There might be some baby ducks,
if the month be June or May.

They really do not talk all that much,
just an occasional quack-quack to say.
They seem to almost go amuck,
during a moment of frolicsome play.

I guess you could call them lucky-ducks,
when they free ride upon the waves.
Up on the shore with their heads neatly tucked,
as they break from their busy day.

I enjoy watching the ducks so much,
I really wish they would stay.
But all of a sudden, we just lose touch,
when they up and fly away.

TITANIC

The great ship went down long ago,
on her maiden voyage was she.
Now she rests far below,
deep beneath the sea.
Yet her worldwide fame continues to grow,
a legend she has come to be.
For her captivating story has let all know,
what a magnificent ship was she.

VICTIM AND SURVIVOR

No one ever calls me sweetheart or dear,
or reaches out to pull me near.

I get no kisses on the cheek,
and no one waves along the street.

There are no congratulations when I do well,
and when I am sick, there are no get wells.

I have been raped, my personality is marred,
and for me making friends is extremely hard.

That unforgettable night when he took me
away,
now affects me greatly most every day.

The nightmares and flashbacks, the distrust and
fear,
bring about loneliness and streams of tears.

Yet I am quite happy, despite it all,
but it would be nice to have friends to call.

Perhaps someday, someone will understand,
and they will reach out and hold my hand.

I once was a victim of a terrible crime,
but I am a survivor and I can still shine.

LITTLE PINK GHOST

Beth needed a costume for the school
Halloween party . . .
She wanted the most beautiful costume that she
could find,
something pretty that would sparkle and shine.
But her parents had no money to spare,
they could not buy her a costume to wear.
Beth knew that it would do no good to sit
around and weep,
so she started to make a costume from an old
pink sheet.
She went to the party as the little pink ghost,
not what she fancied, not even close.
So when the judging of the costumes was about
to begin,
Beth felt saddened and lowered her chin.
Yet everyone else could clearly see,
what the decision of the judges would be.
The little pink ghost stood out from the rest,
the costume was original and it was the best.
So when the little pink ghost took first prize,
no one was taken by surprise.
No one that is, except for Beth,
she was astonished and needed time to catch
her breath.
For her costume was beautiful, so pretty and so
fine,
there was a sparkle in her eyes and she did
shine.

CRITTERS WITH CLOTHES

Why in the world would a pig wear a wig,
just to have hair that is big?
Perhaps as a disguise to pull off a scam,
or maybe the pig is a ham.

Why in the world would a goat wear a coat,
just to keep warm while sailing the high seas in
a boat?
Perhaps the coat was made special for someone
named Billy,
or maybe the goat is just silly.

Why in the world would a mouse wear a blouse,
just to fit in at the White House?
Perhaps to make it easier to get some cheese,
or maybe the mouse is a tease.

Why in the world would a bear wear underwear,
just to keep their bottom from being bare?
Perhaps to make them look innocent and funny,
when robbing the bees of their honey.

Why in the world would a kitten wear mittens,
just to keep their paws from getting frostbitten?
Perhaps to keep their paws purr-fectly clean,
or maybe it is something with purr-sonal mean.

Why in the world would a critter wear clothes?
Perhaps only they would know.

DOCTOR TEDDY BEAR THE COMFORT DOCTOR

Doctor Teddy Bear has been around for many years,
he has dried countless tears, helped conquer childhood fears.
Kept secrets that were whispered in his ears,
and has been there when someone just wanted him near.

He does not put bandages on scratches and cuts,
and he knows nothing about measles, chicken pox and such.
But when it comes to that comforting touch,
Doctor Teddy Bear can do so very much.

When you are in the hospital and filled with gloom,
he can stay with you there in the room.

He will help you relax and will help you rest too,
he can stay right by your side if you want him to.
Your favorite bedtime story will be his favorite too,
so there will be no need to worry about which book to choose.

If you get scared in the night and become filled with fright,
you can snuggle up to him tight until the morning sun shines bright.

They do not wear lab coats and may have
different names,
yet all teddy bears are doctors just the same.

So when looking for a teddy bear,
there is really no need to compare.
Because they all can give you comfort care,
just like Doctor Teddy Bear.

Since the love of teddy bears has greatly grown,
their helpful nature is so well known.
You may already have one of your very own,
right there with you, there in your home.

Pictures of teddy bears are often seen on
greeting cards and balloons,
along with some comforting words like, "Hope
You're Feeling Better" or "Get Well Soon."

So without a doubt, like all teddy bears under
our great sky of blue,
Doctor Teddy Bear really is a comfort doctor and
a very good one too.

WHEELBARROW RIDES

When I reflect upon my childhood and all the
different rides I had,
I realize that there was something special about
those wheelbarrow rides given by Dad.

He would partially fill the wheelbarrow with
autumn's colorful leaves,
then one by one he would lift us in, my little
sister, little brother and me.

We would giggle and grin from ear to ear
throughout each wheelbarrow ride,
he would always tell us to hold on tight, so we
would hold on to the sides.

Those wheelbarrow rides were so much fun, no
other rides could compare,
they were more than just enjoyable rides, they
were precious moments shared.

I thought he could probably move those leaves
faster, if he did not haul us too,
yet I never bothered to say anything, I think he
already knew.

SALTED PEANUTS
(Based on characters created by Charles Schulz)

Due to the passing of Charles Schulz and their recent retirement,
the Peanuts gang was feeling sad and restless and needed some excitement.

So they took a trip to Florida and spent time on the beach,
the salty ocean water refreshed their spirits and provided something special for each.

It was a great opportunity for Lucy to cool off,
to sport the new bikini that she wanted to show off.

Snoopy was out surfing most of the time,
he had Woodstock on his shoulder and a style so fine.

Linus did a little swimming, but preferred just to wade,
what a wonderful beach towel his security blanket made.

Schroeder played his little piano under a beach umbrella,
many were impressed by the talented fella.

Pig-Pen got rinsed off when he took the plunge,

yet he still could have used some soap and a sponge.

Franklin and Rerun played Frisbee on the sand,
they would send the disk flying with a twist of the hand.

Sally made sand castles and played in the waves,
she also collected a pile of seashells that she wanted to save.

Charlie Brown made a sand football,
and even though it was made of sand, he was determined to kick the football once and for all.

So he stuck his tongue out the side of his mouth and made a run for it,
but just when he was about to kick it Lucy ran by and stepped on it.

Charlie Brown fell flat on his back and the football was smashed,
it looks as though he and Lucy will always clash.

Peppermint Patty and Marcie felt sorry for Chuck,
they just hated to see him have more bad luck.

They were sunbathing nearby and had seen what had happened,

they were not surprised though, with Lucy
around it was bound to happen.

Charlie Brown was so humiliated it was making
him sick,
so he ran up to a beach ball and gave it a kick.

The ball soared high and its bright colors twirled,
then it landed gracefully beside a shy little girl.

The ball belonged to her and she was delighted
to have it back,
so she picked it up, ran to her mother and
explained how she had gotten it back.

"Look mommy, that nice boy got my ball back
for me,
the one with the plain round face, see him,
see?"

When the little girl's mother spotted Charlie
Brown there in the crowd,
she waved to him and shouted, "Thank you
young man, thank you, you should be
proud!"

Charlie Brown's face turned red, not from
embarrassment, not from sunburn, but with
pride,
he had never before felt so good inside.

page 4 / Salted Peanuts

Because even though it had happened by
accident, he had finally done something
right,
and that had him feeling more than all right.

He was still Charlie Brown, yet he somehow felt
different,
he had gained an ounce of self-confidence and
to him that made a world of difference.

Of all the Charlie Browns, he will always be the
Charlie Brownest,
but from that moment on, he would do his very
best.

Everyone gathered around Charlie Brown,
they all shared in his pride and shouted, "Happy
retirement Charlie Brown!"

FLAGS ACROSS AMERICA

There are flags across America,
like a great chain of red, white and blue.
They are there for those who were taken,
they are there for me and for you.

Like silent voices the stars and stripes speak out,
some seem to whisper, some seem to shout.

They carry a message across our great nation,
a message that is strong and bold.
It is felt in the hearts of Americans,
Americans both young and old.

It is about liberty, justice and love for our
country,
and it has been known for many years.
So there is no doubt of what the flags are
saying,
the message is really quite clear.

We are proud to be Americans,
that is just how we will stay.
God bless America,
God bless the USA.

WISCONSIN AUTUMN

The days are warm and the nights are cold,
leaves turn to colors of red, orange and gold.

Flocks of honking geese fly overhead,
they are migrating south for the winter ahead.

Squirrels hastily scamper around,
gathering acorns that fall to the ground.

There are bushels of apples and fresh apple
pies,
pumpkins of all sizes and fresh pumpkin pies.

Children play joyfully in piles of raked leaves,
with leaves in their hair and leaves up their
sleeves.

Jack Frost soon nips at your nose,
making it red, as red as a rose.

TOGETHER AS ONE

Let us all live together as one,
all countries, all nations, everyone.

Let us live peacefully like the dove,
replace those feelings of hatred with love.

Let us not waste another precious day,
the hands of time are ticking away.

Let us cherish our planet, our home and each
other,
for we have only one life, there will not be
another.

Let us all live together as one,
all countries, all nations, everyone.

FLY LIKE AN EAGLE

Sometimes I wish I could fly like an eagle,
with my wings spread far and wide.
I would soar high over mountains and treetops,
in the wind, I would let myself glide.
Over waters and valleys, over massive lands below,
I would fly like an eagle with pride.

THE BRIGHTEST RAINBOW

I seen a rainbow too bright to ignore,
I knew that it was brighter than any before.

It appeared in the sky in the usual way,
after a rain on a warm spring day.

The colors were so vibrant, so intensely bright,
no doubt, it was a beautiful sight.

The smell of fresh rain still scented the air,
as I looked in disbelief, just standing there.

Like a giant ribbon it gift wrapped the sky,
it filled my heart with joy and brought tears to
my eyes.

Like the stars and moon, it had a silent voice,
it whispered a message that I heard without
choice.

The message was much more valuable than the
pot of gold,
which can be found at the end of a rainbow, as
we have often been told.

The message clearly said that the universe and
our lives are the most precious gifts,
so let our hearts sing and our spirits lift.

WISCONSIN WINTER

It is cold outside and Jack Frost nips at your nose,
making it red like a winter rose.
Snowflakes gently fall from the sky,
covering the ground with a blanket of snow as the days go by.
Snow banks and snow piles are a common sight,
tree branches are draped with snow like a sugary icing so very white.
Children are busy building snowmen and making snowballs,
sometimes they try to catch snowflakes on their tongues as they fall.
There is downhill skiing and uphill skiing,
sledding and snowmobiling.
Fishermen are ice fishing out on the lakes,
while others get some use out of their ice skates.
Snowplows are out plowing the streets,
snowblowers and shovels are used to keep the driveways and sidewalks snow free.
After being out in the cold, hot chocolate is a great treat,
it warms you up and it is good and sweet.
A Wisconsin winter can be nice,
but use caution when it is extremely cold and be careful on the ice.

WHEN THE ROBINS RETURN

The robins return to Wisconsin in the early
spring,
they fly here from down south with their little
wings.
The beautiful gray, red-breasted birds can be
seen,
before the snow all melts and before the grass
turns green.
You can hear them singing up in the trees during
the day's dawn,
and can later see them out and about in your
lawn.
They are gathering the things they need to build
their nests,
they seem to like dead grass and mud the best.
The robins build their nests with the utmost
care,
they will lay their eggs and raise their babies
there.
A robin's eggs are a pretty light blue,
known as nothing other than Robin Egg Blue.
After the eggs hatch the mother robin feeds
them worms and keeps them warm and
dry,
they grow fast and their mother soon teaches
them to fly.
When the young ones are strong enough they all
fly away,
they will go farther north, and for the summer
that is where they will stay.

EASTER SWEETNESS

A basket filled with colorful eggs, some candy,
some not,
some hard-boiled in a kettle or pot.

Marshmallow bunnies and marshmallow peeps,
sugar coated fun to eat treats.

A chocolate rabbit or a chocolate bunny,
they are so good and yummy.

Chewy, vibrant colored jelly beans,
nestled in Easter grass, some pink, some green.

A stuffed rabbit to hold and cuddle,
they are soft and easy to snuggle.

*MYRON (GRIM) NATWICK**

Many years ago, Wisconsin Rapids was two small cities,
there was one on the east side of the river, one on the west.
Myron (Grim) Natwick was born and raised in Centralia,
which was the city on the west.

Grim was very talented, very artistic,
he gave it his all and he gave it his best.
He became a premier animator and a great cartoonist,
Betty Boop is probably his greatest success.

With her little black curls, batting eyes and her pretty red dress,
she is spectacular and nothing less.
Grim used his gift to create joy and happiness,
he was super spectacular and nothing less.

**Written for the Betty Boop Festival held annually in Wisconsin Rapids, Wisconsin, since 2010.*

VARIOUS TOPICS SHORT STORIES

The Best Christmas Gift is a reflection about time spent with family. The Jealous Fly is about the not so average fly and The Four-Leaf Clover is about believing in you.

The first is suitable for all ages; the other two are suitable for children

Ann wrote the following short stories between 1992 and 1996.

THE BEST CHRISTMAS GIFT

When I was a little girl, Christmas time was the most exciting time of the year.

To me it meant colorful lights, pretty trees, candy, lots of good food, Santa and his reindeer, and most of all, presents!

Of course, like most kids, I wanted toys for Christmas. I would spend hours looking through the wish book trying to decide which toys I wanted so that I could get my list to Santa on time.

Then came the waiting, counting down the days until Christmas. This was the hardest part of all. Believe me; it is not easy for a child to wait for new toys.

Finally, the big day would arrive. It was Christmas!

We would all go to my grandparent's house. Everyone was there, grandma and grandpa, cousins, aunts and uncles, mom and dad, my brothers and sisters and I.

There was always a big dinner and lots of dessert. After everyone was through eating, we would open presents. It was great!

My grandma and grandpa have passed on since

those times and the house had been taken down so that the local paper mill could expand.

I went out and walked through the tall grass recently, where the house once stood. As I walked, I thought about the Christmases that I once enjoyed there.

Yes, the toys were nice, but being there together as one big family, that was the best Christmas gift!

I realize that now.

THE JEALOUS FLY

Most flies are satisfied with the way they look and enjoy their lives . . . but this particular fly became an exception one day when he noticed a butterfly playing nearby.

The butterfly's pretty wings of many colors caught the fly's attention, making him extremely jealous. In fact, the fly was so jealous of the butterfly that he was actually willing to give up his fly body and become a butterfly.

"I am going to become a butterfly, then I too will have pretty wings of many colors!" he said anxiously, and he set out to do just that.

Of course, the jealous fly knew nothing about the making of a butterfly. So the first thing he needed to do was to get some good advice from an expert.

Therefore, he went to the monarch and said . . . "I know I am just a fly but I want to be like you, so could you please tell me how . . . how to become a butterfly?" The monarch spread its pretty wings of many colors and replied . . . "It is not easy to become a butterfly, but if that is what you really want then I will tell you how. First, you have to start out as a caterpillar, then you spin a cocoon and from there you will be born a butterfly."

The jealous fly knew there was no way he could do those things but he still was not going to give up. "There must be another way to become a butterfly", he replied as he went on his way. He went to the bumblebee, the spider, the grasshopper; he even asked another fly. "Could you please tell me how . . . how to become a butterfly?"

They all gave him the same answer as the monarch and that made the jealous fly very sad. He was so sad, he just flew away to find a place to be alone.

Soon another fly came along and asked the jealous fly why he was so sad. So the jealous fly sobbingly told the other fly his problem.

The other fly listened with great concern, then looked at the jealous fly with an assuring smile and said, "Believe me, if you were born a fly you are meant to be a fly and nothing other than a fly. Come with me and I will prove it to you."

So off they flew. The two flies went around the town tasting food and doing all the other fun things that flies do. By the end of the day, the jealous fly was no longer jealous of the butterflies and their pretty wings of many colors. He was very proud to be a fly and wanted to be nothing other.

THE FOUR-LEAF CLOVER

Nearly a year has passed since Mary last competed in the Special Olympics. She is a fast runner and always looks forward to another chance to compete in the running races and possibly win that blue ribbon she has been striving to win for quite some time.

However, Mary was not looking forward to the Special Olympics this year. In fact, she was not even planning on attending.

You see, Mary was well on her way to winning the blue ribbon last year when she stumbled and fell. She scraped both of her knees and even worse, her self-confidence was badly bruised.

Now with the Special Olympics only two weeks away, tears filled her eyes as she stood holding the beautiful frame that she had bought with the intention of some day framing her blue ribbon and displaying it with pride.

However, she had not yet won a blue ribbon and she no longer had the self-confidence to go out and try to win one. At this point, she was actually feeling very doubtful about ever competing again.

Mary had dried her eyes and was putting the frame back into the bedroom closet when her mother came in and said that they would be leaving soon. They were going to meet Judy and her parents at a lakeside park to have a picnic lunch and possibly do some swimming.

Mary and Judy both have Down's syndrome and have been best friends for several years now. They are there for each other through the good times as well as the bad times. They can always rely on each other for good advice and emotional support when they need it.

In fact, on the way to the park Mary realized that this was one of those times that she could really use some good advice and emotional support from Judy.

So, while they were at the park Mary and Judy took a walk together and talked things over. Mary told Judy that she was not planning to compete in the Special Olympics anymore and explained why.

Judy became somewhat upset when she heard the news because they have always went to the Special Olympics together. And although she could understand Mary's feelings, she told her it would be a shame to let the fall she took last year prevent her from ever competing in the Special Olympics again. Besides, it just would not be the same without her.

Judy was able to convince Mary that she should eventually compete in the Special Olympics again, but not until her self-confidence has been restored.

By this time, Mary and Judy had been walking for quite a while so they sat down under a shade tree to rest. They noticed an abundance of clover in the area and thought it would be fun to look for four-leaf clovers. They both know that four-leaf clovers supposedly bring good luck to the ones who find them. And although that may not be true, they thought it would be worth a try.

After looking desperately for several minutes, Mary finally found a four-leaf clover. Since neither one of the girls has ever seen a four-leaf clover before, it was an exciting moment for both of them. They were jumping with joy as they hurried back to the picnic site with the four-leaf clover. They were anxious to show it to their parents.

Mary's mother suggested that something so precious and rare be put somewhere for safekeeping. Since they were planning to stay at the park for quite a while yet, she helped Mary and Judy press the four-leaf clover into the car manual to prevent it from wilting.

By the time they left the park that day, Mary

had decided that she was going to compete in the Special Olympics this year after all. She planned to carry the four-leaf clover in her shirt pocket on the day of the competition, with hopes that it just might bring her some good luck.

Her parents did not see any harm in that since people have always considered numerous items capable of bringing them a streak of good luck. In fact, there were several competitors carrying troll dolls at last year's Special Olympics.

The days passed by quickly over the next two weeks. Mary worked hard at various exercises to help strengthen her leg muscles and improve her running ability.

The big day soon arrived and Mary was so full of excitement she could hardly eat breakfast. She had remembered to put the four-leaf clover carefully into her shirt pocket first thing that morning because that was one thing she did not want to forget.

Mary and her parents were soon on their way. Their first stop was to pick up Judy and her parents. From there, they were off to the Special Olympics at last.

It was a beautiful day for the competition. The

sun was shining in a clear blue sky and there was a soft breeze blowing.

You could almost feel the excitement in the air as everyone gathered for the upcoming events.

The competition was soon underway. With the four-leaf clover tucked safely away in her shirt pocket, Mary now had more confidence in herself than ever before. With the running races about to begin, she was more than eager to get started.

At the sound of a whistle, the running races had begun. The competitors were off to a good start. Mary ran faster and faster and she was soon in the lead. However, in order to hold her position and come in first place, she needed to run at top speed until reaching the finish line.

When she finally did reach the finish line, she was very exhausted and extremely happy. She had come in first place and won the blue ribbon! She ran over to her parents and gave them a big hug. Then she ran over to Judy and gave her a big hug.

However, there was one more thing. She wanted to hold the four-leaf clover for just a moment. As Mary reached into her shirt pocket to get the four-leaf clover, she was shocked to find nothing but an empty pocket. The four-leaf clover was gone! She could not believe it. Somewhere along the way, between all the commotion and excitement, it must have fallen from her pocket.

Mary became sad at the loss of the four-leaf clover because she had grown rather fond of it. She probably would not have won her blue ribbon without it. She later discussed the loss of the four-leaf clover with her parents. They too thought it had probably fallen from her shirt pocket during the competition.

However, even though she did lose the four-leaf clover, it had been a very successful and enjoyable day for Mary. She could hardly wait to put her blue ribbon in the beautiful frame that she had bought for it.

When they arrived back home, Mary rushed into the house to get the frame out of her bedroom closet. On her way through the living room, she stopped to lay her blue ribbon down on the coffee table. To her surprise, there on the floor alongside the sofa was the four-leaf clover. She was picking it up off the floor just as her parents walked in. They shook their heads in disbelief as she stood momentarily cradling it in her hand. They all three agreed that it must have fallen out of her shirt pocket when she leaned over to tie her shoelaces earlier that day.

Therefore, it looks as though Mary won the blue ribbon all on her own. She just needed to learn how to believe in herself.

That evening as Mary and her parents talked about their day over supper, she smiled with pride whenever she looked at the beautiful frame hanging there on the wall, displaying her blue ribbon. And there in the frame alongside her blue ribbon, was the four-leaf clover.

MY POEM FOR ANN

The following poem I wrote shortly after Ann passed away. We were not only sisters; we were also best friends throughout much of our lives.

****

COMPLETELY GRAY

The day my sister passed away,
my blue sky turned completely gray.

There is emptiness in my heart I just cannot fill,
I long for her, long for her still.

Too many poems not written, thoughts not shared,
life on earth is truly unfair.

Some people are taken away way too young,
sketches not sketched, songs not sung.

If I could get her back for just one day,
to tell her I miss her, love her and hope she is okay.

Then maybe, just maybe, for that one day,
my sky would not be completely gray.

AFTERWORD

Ann was not only a poet; she was an amazing artist as well. She could draw both realistic and imaginative things using colored pencils or graphite. She also did some oil painting as well.

Ann held certificates for Basic Art and Fundamentals of Commercial Art, both from Art Instruction Schools.

I now think of Ann as my color wheel in the sky. When I look up at the sunset and see those beautiful, breathtaking colors brushed across the sky, I will think of her.

www.ingramcontent.com/pod-product-compliance
Ingram Content Group UK Ltd.
Pitfield, Milton Keynes, MK11 3LW, UK
UKHW020222250726
13967UKWH00001B/130

9 781105 538810